It was a cool day. Bean was having a snooze under a bush. Jelly wanted to play.

Jelly crept behind the bush. Then she swooped on Bean. "Boo," she said. "Will you play with me?" "No," said Bean. "Shoo. I want to snooze."

Jelly felt gloomy. She sat on the grass. Then she saw a red balloon in the pond. She ran to the pond to get it.

Jelly bent down to scoop the balloon out of the water.   Bang! The balloon popped.

Oops! Jelly fell in the water.

Splash! Jelly splashed in the water. Then she saw a big goose coming across the pond.
"Help," said Jelly. "The big goose will peck me."

She jumped out of the water and she zoomed under the bush.

"Help, help," said Jelly. "The big goose will peck me."

Bean saw the goose coming across the grass.

"Help, help," he said. "The big goose will peck us."

Just then the big rooster ran to the bush.

"Cock-a-doodle-doo," he said. "I will help you. The big goose will not peck you."

So Jelly, Bean and the rooster shouted, **"Cock-a-doodle-doo."** The goose ran back to the pond as fast as he could.

Soon Bean was snoozing again under the bush, and Jelly was happy playing with the rooster.

"oo"

cool	soon
snooze	boo
shoo	gloomy
balloon	scoop
oops	goose
zoomed	rooster
swooped	

cock-a-doodle-doo

High Frequency Words

it was a day play to she the said I in of big and he me you get no on

then saw ran out water just again with could not us will help so back down as wanted jumped